FROM THE EARTH
How Resources Are Made

HOW GEMS ARE FORMED

BY JILL KEPPELER

Gareth Stevens
PUBLISHING

Please visit our website, www.garethstevens.com. For a free color catalog of all our high-quality books, call toll free 1-800-542-2595 or fax 1-877-542-2596.

Library of Congress Cataloging-in-Publication Data

Names: Keppeler, Jill, author.
Title: How gems are formed / Jill Keppeler.
Description: New York : Gareth Stevens Publishing, [2017] | Series: From the
  Earth : how resources are made | Includes bibliographical references and
  index.
Identifiers: LCCN 2015046972 | ISBN 9781482447095 (pbk.) | ISBN 9781482447118 (library bound) | ISBN
9781482447101 (6 pack)
Subjects: LCSH: Gems–Juvenile literature. | Precious stones–Juvenile
  literature. | Geology–Juvenile literature.
Classification: LCC QE392.2 .K47 2017 | DDC 553.8–dc23
LC record available at http://lccn.loc.gov/2015046972

Published in 2017 by
Gareth Stevens Publishing
111 East 14th Street, Suite 349
New York, NY 10003

Designer: Laura Bowen
Editor: Therese Shea

Photo credits: Cover, pp. 1–32 (title bar) Dimec/Shutterstock.com; cover, pp. 1–32 (text box) mattasbestos/
Shutterstock.com; cover, pp. 1–32 (background) Alina G/Shutterstock.com; cover, p. 1 (amethyst) LVV/
Shutterstock.com; p. 5 WPA Pool/Getty Images; p. 6 Evan-Amos/Wikipedia.com; p. 7 Gurov Vladimir/
Shutterstock.com; p. 8 Spencer Sutton/Science Source/Getty Images; p. 9 Joel Arem/Science Source/
Getty Images; p. 11 Bloomberg/Getty Images; pp. 13, 14 (amethyst, peridot), 17 (uncut sapphires) J. Palys/
Shutterstock.com; pp. 14 (garnet), 17 (uncut rubies) Imfoto/Shutterstock.com; p. 15 (main) DEA/Photo 1/
Getty Images; p. 15 (inset) lynnette/Shutterstock.com; p. 17 (uncut rubies) Imfoto/Shutterstock.com; p. 17
(cut ruby, cut sapphire) TinaImages/Shutterstock.com; p. 17 (uncut sapphires) J. Palys/Shutterstock.com; p. 19
(main) Maria Arts/Shutterstock.com; p. 19 (insects) Marc Deville/Gamma-Rapho/Getty Images; p. 19 (statue)
ullstein bild/Getty Images; p. 21 Lionel Healing/Stringer/Getty Images; p. 22 Malcolm Linton/Hulton Archive/
Getty Images; p. 23 Arthena/Wikimedia Commons; p. 25 (main) Patrizio Martorana/Shutterstock.com; p. 25
(inset) David Acosta Allely/Shutterstock.com; p. 27 © iStockphoto.com/ollo; p. 28 Universal History Archive/
Universal Images Group/Getty Images; p. 29 Seqoya/Shutterstock.com.

Printed in the United States of America

CPSIA compliance information: Batch #CS16GS: For further information contact Gareth Stevens, New York, New York at 1-800-542-2595.

CONTENTS

Words in the glossary appear in **bold** type the first time they are used in the text.

BEAUTIFUL AND VALUABLE

They're shiny or sparkly and sometimes very colorful. You might see them in a beautiful necklace, a pair of earrings, or a ring on someone's hand. In some countries, they're even used in objects such as crowns and other special items. They're gems!

But what are gems? Gems, or gemstones, are usually **minerals** that are cut and polished so that people find them beautiful. Often, they're also valued for how rare and durable, or tough, they are. There are thousands of minerals on Earth, but only 100 or so are used as gemstones. Why are they so special?

A SHINY HISTORY

People have used gems for more than 20,000 years! Early gemstones, however, were probably made of organic matter, which means they came from plants or animals. One of these gems is amber, which is usually a golden-brown color and comes from trees. For more on organic gems, see page 18.

People often use gemstones for decoration. The Imperial State Crown of the United Kingdom is set with more than 3,000 gems, including diamonds, rubies, sapphires, and emeralds.

THROUGH FIRE AND WATER

Minerals, including gems, are created in a few different ways. Most are formed below Earth's surface. In fact, some gems are formed more than 100 miles (161 km) underneath our feet!

Some gems are formed when minerals **dissolve** in water near Earth's surface. When the liquid cools or **evaporates**, a new mineral may be left behind, sometimes in the form of a crystal. Most gems are crystals. Gems formed this way will be different depending on what minerals were in the water. When the mineral silica is present, for example, the gemstones amethyst and opal might form.

SWEET SCIENCE

Have you ever tried the tasty treat called rock candy? Then you've actually eaten sugar crystals! Rock candy is made when as much sugar as possible is dissolved in boiling water. When the water cools, it can't hold as much sugar, and sugar crystals form.

Amethysts sometimes form in geodes, which are roundish rocks in which crystals may grow. Geodes are plain on the outside, but can be beautiful on the inside!

7

Heat can be a key factor in how gemstones form. Often, that heat comes from magma, or **molten** rock, that lies beneath Earth's surface. Sometimes the minerals needed for gems are supplied by magma, too.

Gems can form from mineral-filled water that comes from magma. Gems can also be created when rocks interact with heat and pressure deep below Earth's surface. Or magma itself can form gemstones when it cools and becomes solid.

Some gemstones form in the mantle of Earth. They include the gemstone peridot and the most prized gemstone of all. Can you guess what it is?

lava

magma

MAGMA OR LAVA?

Earth is made of layers. We live on the top layer, the crust. Under that is the mantle, which is about 1,800 miles (2,900 km) thick! The mantle is mostly solid rock, but contains pools of magma. When molten rock is under Earth's surface, it's called magma. When it's at the surface, it's called lava.

HOW GEMS FORM

PROCESS

Minerals dissolve in water near Earth's surface.

$\longrightarrow$

Rainwater or water from magma gets into cracks underground.

$\longrightarrow$

Magma gets into holes or cracks underground.

$\longrightarrow$

Minerals in Earth's crust encounter an increase in heat or pressure.

$\longrightarrow$

Minerals within Earth's mantle encounter great heat or pressure.

$\longrightarrow$

RESULT

When the water cools or evaporates, the minerals left behind may be gemstones such as amethysts.

Minerals in the cooling liquid may fill veins beneath Earth with gemstones such as emeralds.

When the magma cools, gems such as rubies may be formed from its minerals.

Minerals may change to gemstones such as garnets in response.

Minerals may change to gemstones such as diamonds in response.

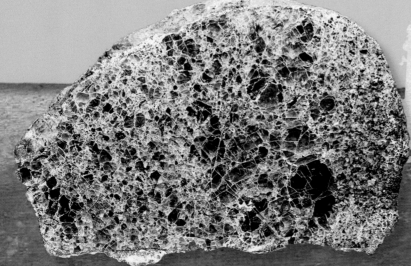

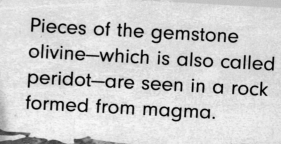

Pieces of the gemstone olivine—which is also called peridot—are seen in a rock formed from magma.

THE TOUGHEST GEM

Diamonds are one of the most popular gemstones. They're formed from the element carbon and are the hardest natural substance known. They're also one of the most valuable. This gemstone takes shape when carbon atoms come into contact with very high temperatures and very high pressure deep underground. The diamonds we see today were formed many, many years ago. They could be billions of years old!

Diamonds can be almost colorless, or they can be colors such as yellow, blue, or black. They can be **transparent** or **opaque**. Most diamonds used as gems are colorless and transparent.

A PENCIL'S SECRET

Diamonds are formed very deep underground. However, the same element that forms this valuable gemstone also forms something else, something you might use every day. Another form of carbon that's found at Earth's surface is called graphite. This element makes up the part of the pencil you write with!

While diamonds are very popular (and can cost a lot of money), they're not the rarest gems. In fact, diamonds are one of the more common gemstones!

A GEMSTONE RAINBOW

While diamonds used as gemstones are often colorless, many gems come in a rainbow of colors.

Rubies are usually a bright red, but range from pale rose to dark reddish purple. They're also called red corundum. Sapphires are corundum stones of other colors, but the most valuable sapphires are pure blue.

Emeralds, which are often bright green, are one of the most valuable gemstones. They're members of the beryl family, along with aquamarines and other gemstones.

Topaz comes in many colors, but is often yellow, orange, or blue. Like a number of other gemstones, it's a silicate mineral, or a mineral containing mostly silicon and oxygen.

MY PRECIOUS!

Many years ago, people started calling gemstones precious or semiprecious. Precious gems were considered the most valuable and rare. Semiprecious gems weren't thought to be as valuable. Many jewelers today don't use these terms. They say the words can be deceptive, because some semiprecious gems are worth more than precious gems.

Gemstones come in many sizes and colors. Even the same kinds of gemstone may come in different shades.

13

Peridot is a gemstone that's often yellowish green in color. Like diamonds, peridot stones are formed very deep beneath Earth's surface. Garnets come in many colors, but are often seen in a deep red variety.

Amethyst is a popular gemstone that can be found in all shades of purple. It's a type of quartz. Opals are the most **delicate** gemstone. They tend to be one base color (often white), but may shine with many other colors. Peridot, garnets, amethysts, and opals are all silicate minerals.

Some lesser-known gemstones are tourmaline, lapis lazuli, jasper, sardonyx, and malachite. These are just a few of the many types.

amethyst   peridot   garnet

WHAT'S YOUR STONE?

There are different lists of birthstones, or the gems connected to the month in which one is born. The list many people use includes these: garnet (January), amethyst (February), aquamarine (March), diamond (April), emerald (May), alexandrite (June), ruby (July), peridot (August), sapphire (September), rose zircon (October), topaz (November), and blue zircon (December).

Most of the world's opals come from Australia. There are a number of different types, including black opals, fire opals, and white opals.

cut opals

CREATING THE COLORS

Gems get their colors from the minerals and elements they're made from. Gemstones that belong to the beryl family are a good example. Plain beryl has no color, but beryl that has iron in it becomes aquamarine, which is a blue-green color. Beryl that has an element called chromium in it becomes an emerald!

Rubies and sapphires are made from the same basic mineral—corundum—but rubies have a small amount of chromium in them and sapphires have titanium and iron. They look completely different! This is also one of the reasons the same gemstones can be different shades of colors.

NOW YOU SEE IT...

Gemstones may have unusual features. Some can change colors. They appear to be different colors depending on what sort of light they're in. The gemstone alexandrite can do this. Cat's eye gems are called that because they have a vertical stripe—like the pupil in a cat's eye! Both are a type of gemstone called a chrysoberyl.

rubies

sapphires

Sapphires and rubies are the same basic mineral, but different elements give them their colors.

FROM THE FOREST AND THE SEA

While most gemstones are minerals, some things we call gems are actually organic substances. These gems were created from living things.

Amber is an example of an organic gem. Humans have used amber for thousands of years. In fact, it may be the first gem used by humans! It's made from resin, a thick liquid that comes from trees. Resin becomes solid over time.

Other organic substances often used as gems include pearls, which are formed by shellfish such as oysters and clams; coral, which is made of the skeletons of tiny sea creatures; and jet, which is formed from fossilized wood.

BLAST FROM THE PAST

Because resin is sticky at first, small insects and other things such as pollen and leaves sometimes become trapped in it. In some pieces of amber, you can still see these things preserved after millions of years! The most valuable pieces of amber may have bugs, such as mosquitoes and spiders, visible inside them.

Amber is actually a natural polymer, or plastic. It can be carved into beads for necklaces. Large pieces of amber have been carved into statues!

FROM THERE TO HERE

To find mineral gemstones, people have to dig into the ground to create a mine. Colored gemstone **deposits** can be hard to find, because gems are often very small and scattered around. It can take a lot of time to find even one gem.

Diamonds can be found in Earth's crust in columns of rock called kimberlite. These columns are known as pipes. They were formed when magma from Earth's mantle rushed toward the surface many years ago, bringing diamonds with it. Mining for diamonds often is done with heavy machinery to break through these rocks.

HUNTING FOR GEMSTONES

There are places where anyone can go to hunt for gems. For a fee, some mines in the United States are open to visitors interested in searching for gemstones. Most gems found at these sites aren't very valuable, but in 1975, a visitor found a 16-carat diamond at a state park in Arkansas!

Gemstone mines can be found all over the world. Most of the world's diamonds come from Africa. This photo shows workers at a mine in eastern Congo.

21

YOU DECIDE

Some people are concerned that gemstone mines may harm the earth, air, and water near their location. Workers can also be hurt at mines if the conditions aren't safe. Sometimes, the workers are young children. In several areas, money from gemstones is used to pay for wars and conflicts in which people are hurt or killed.

Some companies that sell gemstones promise that their stones are "conflict-free." They may also promise miners have safe conditions in which to work and that their mines don't hurt their surroundings.

Do you think it's important for people to ask questions before they make a gemstone purchase? Should a gem's origin matter?

BLOOD DIAMONDS

Diamonds from problem areas are sometimes called "conflict diamonds" or "blood diamonds." Some countries have practices to make sure gemstones are less likely to come from these regions. However, many people don't think these go far enough to help solve the problem.

Diamond mines are cut deep into the ground. They often look like funnels going into the earth.

FROM EARTH OR LABORATORY?

Not all gemstones are mined. Some aren't created in the earth at all—they're created in a laboratory! These gems are called synthetic gemstones.

Most synthetic gemstones have the same physical makeup as natural gemstones. They look the same as well, but they often cost less than natural gemstones. Natural gems are considered more valuable because they're much more rare.

Some synthetic gemstones, such as cubic zirconia, don't have natural counterparts. They can only be made in a laboratory. A white or clear cubic zirconia stone looks a lot like a diamond, but it costs much less.

HIGH-TECH GEMSTONES

Sometimes, synthetic (and natural) gemstones have purposes other than decoration. Gems can be found in lasers, computers, and other technology. Because diamonds are the hardest natural substance, they're sometimes used for drilling and cutting. Even diamond powder can be used for polishing things!

24

This ring contains white cubic zirconia stones. The man-made gemstone can come in many different colors.

BRINGING OUT THE SHINE

When natural gemstones come out of the ground, they don't look much like the gemstones we see in rings and necklaces. Most of them must be cut and polished before they're used for decoration.

There are a few ways gems can be prepared. Some are tumbled in a container with water and a rough material like sand until they're smooth and shiny. Some gemstones are cut with a special saw and other tools. They may be cut so they have a flat bottom and rounded top. Today, most transparent gems are cut with **facets** that make them look even more brilliant in the light.

GEMSTONE ARTISTS

Cutting or preparing gemstones can be an interesting job or hobby. Someone who cuts or polishes gemstones is called a lapidary. The art of working with gems is also called lapidary. Tumbling is considered the simplest way to practice this art. It doesn't take many tools, and young people can learn to do it!

Lapidaries and jewelers use many special tools. They may use a special lens to magnify stones. Tools used to hold tiny gems are important, too!

PIECES OF THE PAST

Gemstones are some of the most beautiful substances known to humanity. They're also some of the most useful. Gems are all around us, whether they're in a ring on someone's hand or in the circuit boards of our computers.

Most natural gemstones were created long ago, sometimes before dinosaurs walked Earth! They're special resources that were formed from a mixture of our planet's own elements and forces. These processes create the features that make gems so striking. People have been fascinated by gemstones for thousands of years—and that's not likely to stop any time soon.

HISTORIC GEMS

Some gemstones are so unusual that they're famous! They may have a special place in history or be among the largest examples of their kind. Perhaps the most well-known gem is the Hope Diamond, a blue diamond on display in the Smithsonian Institution in Washington, DC. This gemstone measures about 1 inch (2.5 cm) long and 0.8 inch (2.2 cm) wide.

Gemstones are used in almost every kind of jewelry. Chances are that someone in your family owns a gemstone!

GLOSSARY

carat: a measure of weight for gemstones

deceptive: leading someone to believe something that is not true

delicate: capable of being easily broken or hurt

deposit: an amount of a mineral in the ground that built up over a period of time

dissolve: to become absorbed in a liquid

evaporate: to turn a liquid into a gas

facet: a flat surface cut onto a gemstone to make it more beautiful

jeweler: an artist who designs and creates jewelry, often with gemstones

mineral: a solid material that occurs naturally, does not come from a plant or animal, and is made of certain chemicals in a certain way

molten: turned into a liquid by heat

opaque: not letting light pass through

technology: the way people do something using tools and the tools that they use

transparent: able to be seen through

FOR MORE INFORMATION

BOOKS

DK Publishing. *Rocks and Minerals: Facts at Your Fingertips.* New York, NY: DK Publishing, 2012.

Squire, Ann O. *Gemstones.* New York, NY: Children's Press, 2013.

Tomecek, Steve. *Everything Rocks and Minerals.* Washington, DC: National Geographic, 2010.

WEBSITES

Gemkids
gemkids.gia.edu
This site provides information on gem terms, jewelry making, and gem types plus many colorful photographs.

International Gem Society
gemsociety.org
Read about the science behind gems and how people study and work with them.

The Rocks Know
scienceline.org/topic/blogs/the-rocks-know/
You can learn about different types of minerals with the Mineral Monday posts.

INDEX